Soul Traveler
A Journey Won

Cossondre Anderson

DEDICATION

I'm writing this to share my truth, to step into my authenticity and to inspire anyone that reads it to know that rock bottom isn't the end, it's the beginning.

CONTENTS

ACKNOWLEDGMENTS

To Ayden, Vincent, Jonah and Aurelia,
I hope you always connect with the magic in the world. I
hope you always know that you are not your emotions, and
that you are so much more than your body.

1 CHAOS

I'm going to take you on a journey with me through space/time and back to former versions of myself. I have always wanted to share this story because it's so unreal even to me, and I was there.

In order to take you through the totally miraculous and parts of my life that were the collision of miracles, destiny and magic, I'll have to start from the beginning which feels really low vibration and airs out a ton of my dirty laundry, so buckle up.

I think it's really fascinating that we all have an inner child that can possess us from time to time. Think about it, when you meet a new relationship prospect, when someone doesn't message you back, when you're sitting alone after a heartbreak. There's a little child inside that screams and cries,

"I'm not enough. I hope I didn't make someone angry. Please don't abandon me."

Well, we are beginning in a space where that child inside of me had full and total control of my body. I've learned over the years to not judge that child, she was learning. If my daughter made some of these mistakes, my words and support to her would be much different than the words and thoughts I have given myself.

I was fifteen when I had my first child. I wanted love so badly, and I had convinced myself that a baby would love me unconditionally, knowing that I totally hated my own parents at the time. We always convince ourselves that someone else can give us what we don't even know how to give ourselves.

I was fifteen, this meant I wasn't old enough to drive, work, literally do anything for this baby. I'll spare you the gory details but within a year my oldest son was living with his older father and grandmother. Would I change it? Probably not because I wasn't capable at the time.

I took this baby on a vacation once with one of my teenaged friends and he got an infection in his neck rolls because I didn't know how to keep him clean and healthy at the time. I don't blame myself; I wish he had a better beginning to this would though because he totally deserves everything in the world.

When I was seventeen, I had a second son, different father. Alex was everything to me. The thing about Alex was that he was a pure soul wearing the mask of heroin addiction. There were so many times I would walk in his shoes and step into this life with him just to connect to him.

The day I found out I was pregnant with his child; I was in the hospital for an overdose. The doctor told me, and I couldn't believe it to the point where I argued her, I just had my period. I certainly knew Alex was not going to believe me. I called him and had him come all the way into the hospital and I had the doctor tell him herself.

Alex was silent for the beginning part of the car ride and then his inner child took over. He threatened to drive us both off an overpass on the highway because he would rather us both die instead.

That was honestly really terrifying for me, but it's interesting how when you're in terrifying or life-threatening situations you can just numb completely and choose to go back and work through it later. I don't know if that's a personal superpower that I have, but during everything traumatic I blanked emotionally.

When my second child was born, Alex wasn't there. He had left to take his friend home. He was really good about missing important things and I still to this day don't blame him for that. Because of his addition, he always said he wasn't going to grow old. I wonder sometimes if it was because of his addiction or just because he knew.

After our baby was born, we stayed together at his parents' house, but I suffered from postpartum depression, and because I was seventeen, I had no idea what that was. All I knew was that I couldn't wake up with my babe, it was difficult to get out of bed, and I was so devastated that I bought another child into the world that I couldn't take care of.

A few months went by, and I started desperately seeking ways to feel better and have hope that things would go a different direction. Alex was sober at the time, to my knowledge, and there was some real potential in those moments. He was working with his dad to buy a house and I started talking about wanting to get married because I wanted a reason to get out of bed now, in my present space.

We snuck away to the courthouse with just our baby in the back of the car and we had this very interesting moment together. Alex and I looked at each other with this gut feeling that we shouldn't go in. I was the only one willing to say it out loud, but he agreed and asked me what I wanted to do. I didn't listen to my gut because I couldn't differentiate feelings of truth and lies at this point. I couldn't trust myself because of a hormonal imbalance post-baby.

Our secret elopement costed Alex his sobriety, both of us a place to live and my son would now start growing without me, another baby without a mom.

Everything you hear is only half a truth. I take this statement so seriously because it is true. Every nonbiased statement is still seen from a perspective in which no one else can access. Every thought, emotion, belief, has come from a space that you are the only one with. Perspective is truly a superpower in itself. It's unique, constructed with portions of empathy, compassion, coldness and intolerance in which the recipe can only be created from the experiences of the person perceiving.

I think that's important to say here. My perspective and the only memories I have of this is through the lens of depression. I don't know the truth of my own life from this section of my memory, and I'm okay with admitting that because the lens of depression kind of looks like a kaleidoscope. You can guess what's happening all day, but you don't really know.

When we lost our place to live, Alex relapse. I relapsed with him because my hands were tied. Alex was usually driving, and I had super poor self-control. Remember this. At this point in my life, when I was in Alex's car, and he drove to get heroin I would do it with him every time because I had nowhere else to go. This is an important detail for later.

My dad eventually let me move back in, and even though I was sober, I was still so lost. When I turned eighteen, I got my first apartment with a roommate, bought my first car on my own and became a stripper so I could afford to do all of that and see my kids.

The money was super good, and I did see my kids. On the weekends I had them and during the week I would go to a rave or two and take e pills after work. This is also important to mention in my story because Alex wasn't the reason I did drugs, he wasn't even around at the time. Shockingly enough, I never really did drugs or drank at work as a dancer, but I spent most of my off time when I wasn't with my kids doing them.

It ended up not working out with my roommate and Alex and I ended up back together. His parents had a rental property where we moved. We basically only had to pay the utilities there, so we moved in and had our child together on the weekends. Our son lived with his parents, which was uncomfortable for me because I could tell they wanted their son to get his life together for this baby, but there was a huge disconnect between them and me. I wanted to do better, seriously. I wanted to be there for my kids at the core of my being. I just didn't know what I had to do to meet that expectation and seemingly everything I tried was not right.

I also didn't know how to be a human being and live my teenaged life and be a good mom. Is there both? I still don't know if there's a way to be both. There probably is but the mom-police wouldn't like it.

In the beginning of moving back in together, Alex didn't want me dancing until he would relapse again. At that point he would want the money. He would find my money no matter where I hid it in the house. Where I worked was a dangerous place to have a lot of cash, so I didn't like taking it there. The club owner offered to let me keep it in the safe there, him and I are still friends to this day.

He's also out of the business now. I love seeing people succeed that come from where I come from, it's a special type of admiration.

2 THE CRAZY

At this point, I started getting friends again outside of my work and relationship life. I needed support and somewhere to go and just be myself where I wasn't catering to men either at home or work.

This is a super incredible space where I met some people who I did plant medicine with and talked about energy, spirituality, quantum physics and learning new things from them. The people my age was in college at this point so I would hang out with them and then go home to my passed-out husband who couldn't hold his eyes open. I was living such a double life, but I found joy and hope in the conversations with these people. Some days, I would do hard drugs just to remind myself that Alex's entire family went insane when he'd relapse. For me, no one noticed.

My family stopped inviting me to holidays like Christmas, Mother's Day, Father's Day. Sometimes the lack of love would eat away at me, sometimes I'd tell myself I did it to myself. I created this mess by doing drugs and having kids. I deserve what I got and now I have to deal with it. Addiction is a tough space to be. The thing you want the most is the thing that keeps you there and it's not the drug, the food, the sex, the alcohol.

The only way to get out is to want something else more. I wanted love. That's all. I wanted Alex to love me enough to get clean, I wanted my parents to love me enough to get me help, I wanted my friends to love me enough to tell me I was going to end up dead. I was possessed by the 5-year-old.

Children need love from other people to literally survive, but adults learn to parent and nurture themselves. I was the small child inside of me that wanted everyone to do it for me because loving myself after everything I had done was too hard.

There are a few times that I wanted to just end it in this space. One time, Alex took a car I had recently purchased out to do something, didn't come back for hours so I knew he was out getting drugs instead. He had pawned the ring I got for me to have a wedding ring. I had to buy it for myself to make myself feel loved and special.

I called him and told him that he had to come back and when he didn't listen, I threw back his entire bottle of Xanax and he found me on the floor. He called 911 and the hospital sent me to inpatient. There was a presence there, I was bunked with an older woman, and something felt okay. I think, to this day, an angel was in that hospital working because what it felt like to be there was unlike anything I had ever felt in my life. I called the older woman after we were released, and she asked me if I felt it. Something was different there and no one could quite figure it out. We felt joy being locked away, we felt hope, connection, happiness. No one did anything to initiate this energy, it was just there.

I went to a friend's house and did DMT, where I saw the light and the dark at war. Beings of love and beings of darkness at war all around me, but also over me and my energy, suddenly at the end of the trip my stomach muscles hardened, and it pushed out love and banished all the dark away.

The next day I found out I was pregnant. Looking back this DMT trip that I had prior to knowing I was pregnant represented what was happening. Holy shit. Alex didn't mind as much this time about the pregnancy, but he did have court pending over his head for assault on me.

We had gotten into a physical altercation, and he accidentally hurt me, more than he intended and I had to get staples in my head. I know it might sound like I'm talking about him like I wasn't a victim of domestic violence, but truthfully, we both were victims of domestic violence. I could have left if I wanted, I never felt like I couldn't. I put my hands on him as much as he did me. It was all the way around unhealthy. I am not a victim; he is not a victim. We made choices that were a direct reflection of us at the time.

I stayed with Alex because if I left and didn't need anyone and got in a healthy relationship that would totally shock my system. I wouldn't even know how to act. Dependency was comfortable, toxicity was comfortable. I stayed because I knew it, I knew how to survive in it, and I could predict what would happen on a day-to-day basis.

Back then, don't get me wrong, I played the victim card. We talked about this, I tried anything to get love. I sold my body for love. I paid the bills for love. I mean the list goes on and on. I did heroin for Alex's love. Not drugs, definitely heroin though because I hated it.

So, back to the story, now I'm pregnant with my third child. Very, very shortly after finding out, Alex gets sentenced to a year in jail for the assault. They had pictures of my head bashed open and blood all over my face that made it look pretty bad. It actually was pretty bad; I just didn't feel like it was pretty bad at the time because I have that blanking superpower but looking back it was pretty bad.

Alex being in jail meant I couldn't live in this house for free, so I went and lived with my aunt who was about 30 minutes away, I didn't have a car at this point, so I was taking 2 buses and a light rail to work. The club owner let me bartend since was pregnant so that was a life saver.

The public transportation system didn't run after midnight and the bars closed at 2am so I made friends with an incredible cab driver that I could trust to take me home. I was saving every dollar that I made outside of diapers for my kids, and I saved the money in one-hundred-dollar bills so I wouldn't break a hundred. It's easy to short yourself fives and tens but you don't really want to break a hundred as much.

The time Alex was in jail taught me that I saved more money and got more accomplished when I was removed from trying to please and get love from others. I didn't recognize this at the time but within months I saved enough money to pay his parents to move back into our house together, I felt too scared to get a place on my own without a roommate yet. I was about twenty-one at this time and his parents allowed my nineteen-year-old cousin to live with me. We cleaned out the house and got the electric turned back on.

As my belly was growing, I started seeing stuff in the house. At night I would see these beings that looked like people but made up of heat waves approach me in the dark. I could feel and see them lean in and touch me. I went down the list of everything I could be seeing including aliens and ghosts. I looked up if there was a weird side effect to pregnancy like the PPD that I didn't know about that could cause hallucinations. I had paranoia setting in because I could see and feel these beings, only at night when it was dark, and I was alone and afraid.

I didn't really have much of a choice but to chalk it up to me taking too much acid or mushrooms or DMT and having some weird permanent effect. I struggled through the entire pregnancy with this, but I ended up living through it to the birth of my baby.

Alex sent me a letter from jail, I still have it to this day. I couldn't believe it when I dug it out and re-read it, but I think these beings were with him too during this time because he wrote me a letter. He told me of a dream he had where I had a daughter, we were alone and struggling and standing in line at social security for some type of benefits or assistance.

We later found out my baby was another boy and chalked it up to coincidence, but don't worry, we circle back to that too.

One night, I remember sitting on the couch. All of a sudden, I was in my head, surrounded by swirls of greys and lavenders, and a being that looked similar to the ones I had been seeing showed me my children. It was a weird form of communication kind of how you'd imagine telepathy, only through thoughts, emotions, images, but I knew it was saying I had to leave Alex to be with my kids. I came to, I was still on the couch. I was confused because it felt like a dream, but I hadn't fallen asleep. Again, I must've fallen asleep, right?

Alex got out two days before I gave birth to my third son and relapsed immediately while I was giving birth. After a year of letters talking about a better life he failed to follow through. This time was much different for me though, because I knew I could live without him.

When I took my baby home from the hospital, I saw one of the energy people in the daytime for the first time. It walked over beside me and leaned over the bed admiring the baby, the same way I was. My son was fast asleep laying on the bed, and I watched this thing I was so terrified of at night lean over my baby and look at him, seemingly with love.

I watched it reach in to touch him like the millions of touches I was familiar with at night, and it gently placed its hand on his leg and at the moment of the touch between them, my child was startled awake. I wasn't crazy, he felt it.

I always called this baby my angel, it was this creation of life that propelled the darkness from me just as the vision I had on DMT moments before learning about him. My cousin was still staying with us at the house, I left my newly born infant son with my teenage cousin and worked as a stripper 14 hours a day, every day, until we had enough money to move out.

My cab driver that I had been using for the last year was driving me every night and I was keeping all my cash on me so that Alex couldn't steal it or hunt it down. He knew I was saving and working so much so I'm sure he was hunting for it.

I would show my cab driver how much I had been saving, he would let me sit in his front seat and smoke cigarettes and play EDM music. This man was another guardian angel. I didn't get kidnapped or raped selling my body in Baltimore city all day every day. He yelled at me for having that much money on me in the city. I told him about my husband and how I had to leave and been working so hard to take care of my infant.

He was there for me; he was the consistent face I had during that time. Everyone who works in strip clubs uses a fake name for their safety. My cab driver knew my real name, we had become close friends almost in our daily drives home. He would let me hang out and drive with him to drive other late-night workers home sometimes.

His name was Mike and I still think about him regularly, I hope he's doing okay. I hope his life is amazing.

I lived most of my life never feeling safe. There were few moments in my life that I felt safe and loved. With Mike, I always felt that.

Eventually, I had enough money (I think it took me two weeks) to start looking for an apartment for my cousin, my baby and myself. I was looking on backdoor websites because I had no credit and no bank account. I wanted to pay cash every month and I was terrified, but I was going to make it happen. I had a plan that every month I'd save all the bill money before spending anything. I still didn't even have a car and neither did my cousin, so I was looking with access to bus routes and ways to get to work safely.

I found a little apartment created out of the top floor of a town home and went to see the place. The landlord's name was Ken and he actually lived in the bottom floor. The rent was $850 per month, two bedrooms, a bathroom, a living room. It was small but Ken was nice, and I felt safe there.

I told Ken that I was a stripper downtown, I didn't have proof of income or a bank account, but I could pay the rent and give him the deposit right now. He said he would do it for 3 months up front, but he would have to talk to his wife. He said his wife was out of town and if she comes back and finds out he moved a stripper in she would be super suspicious. I mean, yeah, I would be too.

A couple days later I got the call and Ken decided to rent me the apartment. I went to work to get some money to move and, on the way, Mike says,

"How's the new apartment? Did you move in yet?"

"How did you know I even found one, I was about to tell you!"

"I have a good friend; he calls me the other day and tells me that he has a stripper from the block trying to rent the apartment upstairs, but he doesn't know if it's a good call with no proof of income. I asked him what her name was, guess what he told me?"

"No, way."

"He told me her name was Cossondre, could you believe that? I told him that you would always pay the rent, that I had been driving you for a year and seen you stacking all of your cash for a better life."

Miracles aren't people having superpowers or coming back from the day. It's not witchcraft, energy work, aliens. Miracles are moments where something is impossible, shouldn't happen by all standards and methods of measurement, but they do anyway. Mike was my miracle.

3 THE EGO

Things were looking so bright, my cousin's dad gave us a pickup truck, we moved to our new space. My other children could come over every weekend. Alex's parents let me get my middle son more often because there wasn't drugs or violence in the house. Things were really exciting.

I started losing more weight to make more money at work. In the clubs that I worked in the tiny girls made the most money from regular customers. I was eating a lot less and my body and the money and the safety of my new apartment started getting to my head a little. I was all business at work though. I upsold everything I could, and I knew how to compromise well.

Because of the work I was doing I would go get STD tests pretty regularly, even though I used protection always. One morning I had to go downtown and do this, and I was early for work, but I just went in early so that I could get ready for the day there. I was at a new club and the owner lived out of town and rarely came into the building but again, the hands of fate run rapid in my life and on this very day of my appointment he was there, and we met.

Let me remind you here that there are only perspectives and never truths so that I don't get sued.

For the purpose of not using names, we are going to call this club owner "E."

E never went back into the club for that trip, but he took me to dinner, he stayed on a boat in a marina which I thought was super cool. Walking to it at night definitely reminded me of a serial killer show I was a huge fan of watching, until I was walking down a dock at night with a stranger.

That night he gave me a thousand dollars to buy a MacBook for college. I told him I had recently enrolled, I actually had, and how I was trying to use this job to really do the right thing.

We met another time before he left and this time I slept over. I was leaving in the morning, and he was in the bathroom and as I walked out the door, I noticed a huge stack of money to my right completely not observed.

I had heard of rich guys doing this. They leave a ton of money out to see if you'd steal it, I wouldn't have stolen it anyway, but they typically determine trust that way because people use them for money so often. I later found out that it was exactly that, a test.

E wanted me to stop dancing and bartend, I did. He bought me two cars over the course of our relationship. About six months into dating, I found out that he was married. I never interfered in his married, but I actually did develop feelings for him.

Partially because it was kind of forced on me. I remember when he said I love you, he kept saying it consistently, I wasn't ready to say it back, but he'd repeat it over and over almost like programming my subconscious to believe it.

I later learned about the brain, the subconscious and how to reprogram my own brain, and how it had been programmed. E did a lot of programming. Do I think he knew he was programming me? Yes and no. E really liked games, he made everything a game. He would play games and see if he could get women to do certain things, wild things, what it would take, what made them tick. I think he learned what buttons people have by playing distorted games with people.

Over the years we were together he took me to complete my current bucket list. I was going to school and running his club but eventually I had to drop college to run the club. It made me feel really good to have access to a lot of money, new things, be running a business, feel good about my body. I was getting the love I had been chasing for so long, the problem was, it wasn't love. Attention isn't love. I had to learn that through this experience. Money, wealth, sex, attention, material or name brand shit, none of that is love.

Something thar never sit right with me was part of the job of running the club involved hiring very young girls. Recruiting them the way that the army makes promises to young men who end up depressed and suicidal.

My job was to mislead them. I made ads for shooter girls per E's request, we had no shooter girl position. We get them to walk around in their underwear and get guys to buy them drinks until eventually they were doing private rooms and selling their soul for cash.

I know from being on that side of the bar that even on drinks guys would try to stick their fingers anywhere they could. Your body was your business in this industry no matter how you chose to use it.

I could make the club run, manage the money, train the people but recruiting is the thing I will never sit right with. I hired a girl; I will never forget her name. Jessica Christina Leatherwood. She was 18 years old. She was gorgeous and just such an incredible soul. The industry killed her before her ninetieth birthday. Very young girls are highly susceptible to ending up dead in motel rooms in Baltimore.

I loved Jessica. I took her on some of my bucket list ventures with me. I really felt awful the moment I would meet these young girls because I was the person who was ripping their potential from them, and in some cases their lives.

There was a moment here when I had another dream-like vision similar to the one I had when I was pregnant. This time I saw E and myself in a hotel room, I remember the walls were a scarlet red and the lamps were oddly shaped. This time I know it wasn't a dream for sure because I was driving on a highway. I started to notice with these visions or connections of some sort that time was functioning differently. I had seen an entire scene play out between E and I, what felt like a 10-minute scene except I was only not present behind the wheel for what seemed like three seconds. I refer to this as dream time a lot. How you have an entire dream play out like a two-hour movie, but you've only been asleep for a few minutes.

A few months later, E and I decided to go to Atlantic city, but our usual hotel was sold out along with most of the hotels in the area. We ended up staying at a new place in a new location. This location was the same one from my vision months before, but a different scene played out because I was pregnant. In the vision I saw E leaving his wife, but I was pregnant, and it wasn't E's baby, but we remained friends for this off period.

When I went home, I started seeing shadow people out of the corner of my eye. Sometimes I would see features, I was always afraid of intruders more than spirits because I was a single mom. I had a roommate in this house who was also a single mom. I took a nap one day while my kids were in school, and I had a dream.

I dreamed that I was in a school that had an active shooter. I started crawling down the halls so I could play dead in case I bumped into them, and I get to the end of a hallway and see a little girl at the end with blonde hair and freckles. She has her hands behind her back and looks scared. I look up and ask if she's okay or if she needs help. She dropped the gun from behind her back and I woke up. Bleeding.

I felt like this was my body telling me the baby wasn't going to work out, or the baby telling me there was something wrong with it, or a spirit guide telling me we sacrifice one to save many. I don't know, but no matter how sure you are that something wasn't right it doesn't make the loss of a child any easier.

Just for kicks, I opted to miscarry at home and my uterus decided to hemorrhage blood. I couldn't even drive to the hospital I was expelling blood at such an insane rate. I laid in bed with a towel with my youngest son who was about three at this time. I wanted to lay with him until he fell asleep before I called an ambulance. I didn't want him to see them take me out with flashing lights. Finally, he was asleep, just before I passed out, I called my roommate upstairs and told her to take the baby up to bed and then call 911.

I needed some work and a blood transfusion, but I carried on.

During this time, Alex met another woman who was a counselor at one of his rehabs. They had gotten together, her life spiraled straight downward, and I had heard they were robbing people. He always wanted to be Bonnie and Clyde, but I wasn't a fan of jumpsuits and chains.

I used to let them come babysit the kids while I would work sometimes, at this point all of the kids were back with me in my home. I went and bought key locks for the bedrooms and locked up all my valuables in order to have them stay. One of our kids had a Nintendo console go missing in that time and I was missing several spoons. The last time I let them watch the kids, Alex told me that his girlfriend was pregnant.

He asked if I was going to be angry if it was a girl. I said I wouldn't be. I have my kids and I'm taking care of them. He never was asked for child support, he was never asked to support the kids in any way at all, the only reason I let him babysit and locked up all our stuff was for the kids to know him. I wanted them to know him.

After the miscarriage I tried to work it out with E. E could be really controlling at times. He talked about sex 24/7 and when I was with my friends, he'd want me to send him naked photos all of the time. He still lived out of state with his wife, and it was hard for me to base my life around his texts and phone calls. It gave me a guilt that I had to be talking about sex during my time with my kids and it was starting to become embarrassing with my friends.

I started getting drunk at work and driving home. I cut all my hair off, I wanted freedom. I felt suffocated. He used to make jokes that I was getting too old for him, but I don't think they were jokes. He wanted the tiny 18-year-old girls working at the club, that's what made money because that's what he liked, and I started to realize I looked like a fool. He was coming into town and not telling me he was there, carrying on relationships with other people, putting my body at risk for STDs, and ultimately left me for an 18-year-old girl.

I reflected on this a lot. Where to go from here, I knew this day was coming. How can I leave, not only this business that belongs to my ex, but the strip club industry entirely?

They don't joke when they say it's hard to leave that industry. It's also hard to find your self-worth that isn't in material things like money, brands, or looking hot.

When I cut my hair, I knew it was over with E. Maybe I cut it so that I could force it. Maybe I cut it to prove that what we had wasn't love, it was superficial. I knew I needed to figure out a new plan for my life, but I had no direction on where to go from here and I forced it because I knew I needed out, but I didn't have the balls to leap out of my career, financial stability, everything.

E was so good at pushing people's buttons that when his wife found out about us, she did everything to save her marriage. We went on vacations all together, we hung out together. While we were hanging out E was with other girls.

Anyway, his wife helped me out. She agreed to cosign on a lease across the country and I would start over with all my kids. She started making a plan around then for herself too, I think. She's remarried now and happy. She really is a pure soul. She tells me happy birthday every single year on my birthday, still to this day.

I didn't even think about how terrifying it would be starting over in a new place with no one and just my kids, I figured I'd invite a friend on an adventure, and we would work it out. I was determined to shed this misery I was choosing to live in for financial comfort.

I tried not to judge wealth, but it happened kind of organically. I didn't like who I had turned into with money, I didn't like what money made these girls do. There are spaces of existence on this Earth where people do insidious things for money. Nothing beats what you're willing to do to yourself if you're in that space. The damage is very difficult to repair.

If you are in this space and you don't know how to get out, just take the leap, it always works out. Maybe you'll have a Mike, or maybe you can make it happen on your own. My point is challenging doesn't mean impossible.

4 THE AWAKENING

The day I was leaving to move was hard. I took all my children with me, except my oldest son. I had arranged for his father to move into my old house so that his life wouldn't be uprooted. I even cosigned the lease for him.

I had a bank account and credit at this point. I had taken money from my last day at the club from the safe. I loaded up my dog and my kids and we hit the road. We were traveling with two of my friends and the trip was long and tiring. We got there sometime the next day, I got the keys and I jumped into the pool in the back with my clothes on.

It was the biggest house I'd ever lived in, and that was the only day I tried not to think about work, what to do, how to make enough money without becoming a stripper in the new place.

I asked my two roommates together to pay half the rent. Each bedroom one quarter of the rent. This would leave me enough for food and utilities. I paid for two rooms, me and the two boys. They should each pay their own room.

One of them went on to be quite successful. Probably more successful than I had ever seen him, and he just kept climbing the ladder to success. I think he needed the new chapter as much as I did because he surely didn't waste it. He and I both slipped back into old patterns a couple times but ended up parenting ourselves back into the right mentality.

My other roommate, she didn't get a job. She moved into the third roomie's room and screwed me over a few times. Eventually, we all felt it best after a few substantial confrontations to part ways and they moved into an apartment together.

I had a friend for ten years that moved in from back home, she wanted to move, and her house was getting foreclosed on. She shared my love for spirituality and some of the best conversations we had were about meditation and growth.

When she moved in, however, she took over the house and because I felt alone and co-dependent I struggled to speak up. When she moved in, she threw a lot of my stuff away, sippy cups for my kids. She also had a son and we tried parenting together, but I really wasn't vibing with my kid's newfound expectations and behaviors.

My kids would fly back home sometimes, they would fly unaccompanied and visit their grandparents. Alex's parents. On one of these trips back home, my roommate's daughter was supposed to fly with them back. She ended up getting a last-minute job interview for a job she really wanted, so I booked a flight to go get my kids.

I was dating a girl at the time, and she was going back home for Thanksgiving or Christmas, I can't remember the holiday. She was super sweet, I actually really liked her. Don't worry this is all relevant.

When I got into Baltimore, I rented a car and Alex had called me, I hadn't seen or talked to him for a while, but he needed a shoulder. His girlfriend apparently left him. I had been in another state focused on me, work, the kids that we ended up hooking up. Just the once.

When I got back home to my dad's house for the night, I laid on the couch in the basement to go to sleep. I felt my ovary throb.

No. Fucking. Way.

Yep. I knew that moment.

They say that women know their bodies and are just often disregarded, told it's in their head or made out to be crazy. I can't speak for all women, but I knew. I knew that day.

I went back to my new home with my kids. Alex's grandfather has passed away recently. I couldn't tell my roommate I was pregnant yet, because quite honestly, I didn't even know what I was going to do, and I also had no actual evidence aside from a gut feeling and me seeing shit again.

I started seeing a man pace the hall between the living room and the bedrooms. I ignored this for weeks upon weeks. Finally, I'm sitting in my bed one night and I see the heat wave person approach my bed. It honestly seemed a little hesitant.

At this point in my not-so-hallucinations, I'm like fuck it right. I'm sitting in mt room talking to it. I asked if it was who'd been seeing in the hallway, it didn't talk back but I just knew.

I asked who it was, again, I just knew it was my children's grandfather. This is on my in-law's side, mind you, so I'm already not a fan of where this is headed.

He wanted to tell his wife that he was okay, and he loves her. He really needed her to know. Again, no words but I could feel it. I could feel the pain and importance.

I'm straight up like,

" I can't tell them that I'm talking to you, they're never going to believe me."

Suddenly, a flash of imaged through my mind of all these different necklaces. I had no idea what necklaces, but he was basically trying to say just tell them you know about the necklaces,

Seriously? I'm thinking. I call my mother -in-law the next day. We've never been close. I say, I had a dream. I have to say I had a dream because then I don't sound like a rambling lunatic, right? Okay, I tell her all this shit but in dream format. Rolling with the dream story. I get to the necklaces; I start crying hysterically what the fuck is happening to me. This man's emotions are literally rolling through my body like I'm him.

Turns out, when he died the whole family had necklaces made with his fingerprint on it. I had no idea. His wife called me and wanted to know more, like what he looked like in my dream. I couldn't tell her it wasn't a dream. She was very catholic, but she believed me. She said she had experiences through her life too, clear knowing. She's a claircognizant.

Back then I didn't think you could be spiritual and believe in God, that there was no overlap. I've come to learn much different in recent years, I've come to realize you can only have these experiences for so long before you end up being brough to God at some point. Whether you want to call him that, or source, or whatever. There's a consciousness here that created us, that's inside of us, I don't know exactly how it works but I know it's there.

I didn't have the opportunity to tell my roomie about my pregnancy before she found out on her own. She was really mad and basically said she wasn't going to help raise another kid, I didn't blame her so I asked my mom to move down when my lease was up so I could figure this our once and for all. I really loved it where I was, and I wanted to make it work.

My roommate was a registered nurse and I think that's super important to mention because she didn't start looking for a job before the lease was up, so she was unable to get her own place. My mom and I downsized space so she would be moving into my room and leaving pregnant me on the couch. She also didn't pack her stuff in time to move and I had to pay a pro-rated fee.

She never said sorry. I started paying attention to the woman that I looked up to in my life and who I compromised parts of my own well-being for, and she never said sorry. She made friends with my old male roommate, and they would gossip about me and my mom, and then a couple days after moving in, I got a call.

My kids had just come home from a trip to Baltimore the day before, but Alex's mother was calling me. She was screaming and crying. It was the call we all kind of knew would come and it was the biggest fear really.

Alex died; he took his own life.

I might have gone into shock after that, I had to tell my kids and get to the airport with them and leave. I told my roommate and my mom, and I had to tell my kids. My roommate was supposed to be going out, so I went into my kid's bedroom and sat waiting for her to leave. When I heard the door close, I told my kids.

Of course, the door swung back open and while I'm hold my kids crying I have her passing by. I just wanted space. I was about to have a baby in a month who was never going to meet her father. I couldn't even feel that pain yet because my kids needed me to be strong, to feel their pain.

They always hoped he would get better, there were a lot of "one day," ideas and hopes that were burning in their hearts.

There was this pattern and lack of boundaries on my behalf, but when Alex died, I had a concrete wall of boundaries. I stopped hugging my friends, I stopped any type of physical affection because one touch would make this endless black hole of pain erupt.

I spent a week with his parents. We saw the body before it was cremated. His girlfriend at the time left rehab to come to his funeral, she didn't get the news in time for her to see him gone.

Seeing his bod was hard. He was in the back of a room, not in a casket but on a stretcher. It was a room in a funeral home, the room was so long that I had only mentally prepared myself to go a short distance.

I was due to give birth next month, and we were walking in with his two older brothers and his parents. His older brother and I stopped halfway to where he was. It felt for a moment like we connected and just knew that going further would be more difficult. He looked at me and nodded in a reassuring way, almost saying he understood. There was a couch halfway where I think his brother stayed, I took a breath and kept walking. When I got to the body, I swore I heard his voice in my head saying he really did it this time.

A month before this moment I was in Baltimore visiting. I remember driving near my dad's house and getting this gut wrenching feeling something would happen to Alex. I called him; we hadn't talked in months even though I was pregnant. We weren't on the best of terms, so when I called, he was surprised. I asked if he was okay, where he was staying, if he had a bed to sleep in because I remember that when I didn't have a bed to sleep in, when I had nothing, I wanted to die.

It's like I knew it was depression and not just the drugs. He ended up blowing me off, making me sound silly for calling but he always knew I was a little more connected than he would ever admit.

When I got pregnant with Aurelia, the actual visit that it happened, he asked to drive my rental car. I let him. He took me downtown to get drugs. He wanted me to do them with him, I don't think I ever told anything that. I wasn't driving, he repeated the same circumstance that worked on me so many times before.

This time when he got his drugs, when he pulled over on an ally to do them, I got out of the car. I got out of the car, in a short dress in the middle of a dangerous part of Baltimore city. I stood on the street in the cold and waited.

When he was done, I got back in and dropped him off and went home. I made choices the last year that could've maybe changed his outcome, prolonged his life, given him hope like the times my depression kicked my ass and I would've done anything for hope. I think when he did that, he was looking for love or hope. Maybe I think that because that's always what I was looking for, it could just be a mirror of my own past.

When we went back home, I was preparing to give birth. I spent a week in a house full of people grieving Alex. I helped clean and wash his old belongings, found hidden old needles and cans in the guest room of his parent's house. I even went to see the place where he was staying. I won't describe it to you, I don't feel that would do anyone any good, but let's just say he didn't have a bed. He lied.

I started seeing Alex in mirror reflections, seeing shadows in my rearview mirror at night, feeling paranoia, feeling constant anxiety. I came to realize that it was Alex's emotions going through me like my first spirit experience did but at the time I felt like I was getting paranoid schizophrenia.

Did you know that there are a lot of links between Schizophrenia and the possible experience of something more spiritual and profound? I feel like I could've totally been diagnosed with paranoid schizophrenia and went down that road, but I had to yank myself out of it.

I'd have dreams of Alex coming to me for help crossing over, he'd take me to places he was. Once he told me he thought he was in hell, I told him he wasn't, and he had to keep going. I think when you don't battle your demons in your human life you have to battle them in the end to become at peace.

After about 10 months of dreaming of his crossing over process, I dreamed of him on a beach. I got a phone call from his girlfriend asking me about a dream she had of him. I will never forget it because days later she also died. I felt like he was coming to show her he was okay, that she was okay and not to have guilt. Now I almost wonder if he was coming to great her for her departure.

I hadn't yet grieved this, this whole time I was holding it in, supporting everyone else, taking care of my infant daughter- OH.

Remember that letter he wrote me? How he

dreamed of me with a daughter waiting in line at social security, alone and struggling? Yeah, I gave birth 4 weeks after he died. I had to take my infant daughter to social security in order to add her to his death benefits. I was shocked we were eligible because he never really worked, but apparently, he filed taxes every year.

I often wonder if he dreamed that he died too, that he didn't mention that. Maybe it was a random flash.

After his girlfriend died, I wanted to move back to Baltimore. I needed space to grieve, and I was struggling across the country. It was a tiny house I could barely afford, I needed to go to where I knew how to make money and could grieve this.

No one wanted me to uproot my kids again, they said I moved too much, they said I was inconsistent and unstable. They were hypercritical on my parenting, so I stayed.

If there's one sure thing, I have learned through the entirety of my life is that when I get a gut feeling I need to do something, I should do it even when it doesn't make sense because fate runs rancid in my life, and I will eventually get forced in that direction anyway.

We got bed bugs, so I ended up back in Baltimore but instead of in a house, in my dad's basement and instead of having belongings, we had nothing.

5 SOULMATES

Moving back to Baltimore was emotionally difficult because we lost everything. I was another huge hit to my ego, another thing I failed at. I kicked myself for once again listening to other people over what was coming from within me, my own intuition traded for exterior opinions and perceptions.

The wound from Alex dying that had never been grieved or released grew outward like a plague infecting everything it touched. I mean everything.

There are moments when the universe, spirit, God, whatever is trying to steer you and when you don't listen for so long and finally get forced there tends to be an array of immediate and good things that happen.

I always imagine this as some kind of backed up abundance that was waiting for you, but you were too scared or stubborn to go get it.

When I moved into my dad's I had a career move waiting for me that was not in the strip club industry. It was a really incredible job aiding to teach children with autism. It actually substantially impacted my parenting, especially with the baby.

I learned a ton about positive reinforcement, negative

reinforcement, behavior extinction and applied it to the overall human psyche. When I learn something there's no limit to what it can be applied too. Creating behavior extinction is the same for a small child as it is for an ex-boyfriend or girlfriend.

Within a month of moving into my dad's basement, sharing a room with all of my children and having a friend watch my beloved dog, I checked my bank account one morning and the balance read $10,000.00

Like any sane person, I thought this couldn't be right. Someone must have mistaken an account number and it would obviously need to be taken back,

Turns out, I call the bank and the money was mine. A totally unexpected and substantial deposit to my account.

I was standing in front of my stepmom when my mouth hit the floor and something I will never forget her saying was something I had heard before from someone very dear to my heart.

"This always happens to you; your life doesn't function on the same playing field as everyone else's."

I had a friend that I would tell my experiences to, and this is just a short compilation of them. He used to always tell me my life didn't play by the same rules as others. I don't know if that's true because I am only living in my own shoes but in my experience of knowing people, everyone has this ability to connect to everything around them.

My perception, and again let's remind about perception here. The perspective I hold is that when you are willing to perceive the world differently, things start happening. Unexplainable things. I have lived on the side of living a magic-less life, yet as I have just told you, the magic was always there. I just started noticing it.

The more it came to the forefront of my awareness the more strength the connection would emit. Even in my depression, PPD, I had the gut feeling not to get married and I ignored it because I was trying to get something. Lack is a low vibration.

I used the money to move out of my dad's house and get my dog back, refurnish the house with our belongings. It was almost as if we had lost nothing at all. I actually did my space up in my ideal image with matching furniture and a corner shelf filled with plants.

I loved waking up in the morning and I was finally safe. My kids were safe, the bills were paid, I was safe. My cousin even moved back in with me when I came home, the one that helped with my son when I left Alex. Honestly, another angel in my life.

Once my subconscious finally deemed the struggle gone, the kids settled and me safe, all of those years of emotion from Alex dying finally surfaced. I lost about 70lbs and didn't work out at all. Depression got so bad that I was mentally ill.

I was working the job at the school and absolutely loved it, I met someone there named B. I was drawn to B and I knew this was a totally fucking stupid and irrational attraction. What did I say? I was going to follow where I was lead. Well, long story short, I had to resign from my job that I actually loved because of a situation with B.

B had begun staying my house, he didn't contribute any way financially, never cleaned, never did anything for anyone else really and his judgement of the type of person you were, was based on what you did for him. I let this go on until one specific day.

I had read something about Opalite that stuck with me. I used to have one hanging in my car until one of the kids asked me what Opalite was for, and I used the handy-dandy Google to learn that Opal and Opalite is used to propel you into your purpose, on the right path. It's like a tornado that swoops in removing everything that doesn't belong and getting you where you need to be as fast as humanly possible.

I had got this Opalite right before we got the bed bugs and had to move home. It had been hanging in my car this entire time. When I got tired of B and my intuition wasn't nudging me to hang around him anymore, I put the Opalite under his pillow.

A couple things happened following that, but I ended up leaving the job and he ended up abruptly leaving my house.

I probably would have stayed at that job forever. Fate, destiny, whatever, I'm glad I listened this time. My depression got worse after B and being jobless, but my bills were always guaranteed paid because of the death benefits from Alex.

I had emotions pouring out of me from his death, seeping from my pores. Thoughts I had like,

"No one will love me; I have four kids."

"I'll be single until I die, he left me here to take care of them on my own."

When the hope that he would never get sober or get better left it left me so sad. I haven't even touched on the survivor's guilt yet. Alex and his girlfriend both died 10 months and 10 days within each other. Isn't that curious? An angel number apart.

It left me with this pressure to not die too or my kids would have no one, it left me with a pressure to make sure they knew all the good things. There was so much pressure it was crushing me and the one thing I wanted was keeping me there again, love.

Did you know that emotions are stored in your organs? Emotions are literally just energy. When you spend time learning about energy because you tend to naturally channel it from all around you, you learn a lot of really cool things. For example, depression energy is stored in the gallbladder.

I got a new job bartending really close to my house and thankfully not in a strip club. I didn't really need the money, but I wanted to meet people and get out of my house. I only worked for a couple months before I got really sick. My gallbladder needed to be removed and with four kids you have to plan an entire vacation to get to the hospital.

Nobody ever thinks about that when you have kids. Having to call an ambulance and wait until your child is asleep or having to plan childcare for a hospital visit. My mom was out of state, she went back to the country to be with her parents as they got older and so I had to depend on my stepmom and mother-in-law mostly.

I looked like skeleton from my depression and then the puking by the time I got to the ER. I made it a point to get the morphine, look I had been sober. At this point a little morphine and a hospital vacation wasn't hurting anyone.

Get this, because I had to be out of work for another six weeks, they had to get someone else to cover the bartender shifts until I came back.

I started really deep diving into my spirituality during this time. I was journaling, meditating, and watching transformational speakers non-stop. I healed some layers around my mom, broke up with some former versions of myself. I decided that I wasn't going to believe no one was going to love me anymore.

Wait, with my gallbladder gone I really started feeling better. How validating is that with the depression energy storage thing? I knew it probably needed to be removed from the depression but didn't realize until now how immediately I felt better.

Anyway, I decided I wasn't going to believe no one would love me. I wasn't going to believe that I would have to settle or compromise anymore. I wrote a list of things that I truly wanted and needed in a partner (this doesn't work if you're a Leo) and I decided that I was going to start asking out every cute guy I saw so that I wasn't afraid of rejection anymore.

The best way to conquer your fear is consistent exposure. I used to be terrified of a lot of things, normal things. I was afraid to go live on Facebook, so I did a 52-day live challenge for myself. Anything you haven't done before feels uncomfortable until its practically routine.

I started asking cute guys out. Every single one I saw, and I was terrified every time. Guess what? I didn't conquer my fear of rejection at all because not a single one said no. I was shocked but also I did get super comfortable making the first move and just saying how I felt or what I wanted.

I think it's super important for people to be able to speak what they think, what they feel, what they want and do it confidently and in their power.

Another thing I did during this time was love myself. Every single thing that I wanted a partner to do for me, I found the boldness to provide for myself. My cousin helped with the children which allowed me some space to flow with this.

I had some pretty contradicting things on my list of an ideal partner. I had

- Must like kids
- Doesn't have kids
- My ex-in-laws like him
- Doesn't want any more kids
- Likes animals and pets

I don't remember the entire list, but I know those things were on it. I remember thinking about the kid thing and thinking that I wrote down some pretty improbably combinations in a person.

When I went back to work bartending, I met him. He had begun bartending while I was gone, I think. He was super shy, totally adorable. His name was Kevin, and I didn't talk to him for a while because I thought he was a lot younger than me, but it turns out he was older. I had dropped my expectations of what masculinity needed to be, my definitions of men weren't working anyway, and I was ready for someone good. Someone that was in alignment with the direction that I was headed and not who I had been.

My bedroom at this house had a sliding door with a deck off of it. The kids never had to see him, and he would come over at night and we would watch movies I hadn't seen. My soul let out a sigh of relief when we got together as if it knew and had waited for him for so long.

It might not make sense, like most of this book, but it also might make the most perfect sense. I can't explain it, but I just knew right away that he was the one I was supposed to be with. I felt the relief like this whole time my soul was looking for him.

I wanted to make sure that all my cards were on the table, I was clear and upfront about what I wanted. I was clear about my situation and when I told him about Alex, he was able to put together that he actually went to school with Alex. His parents actually knew Alex's.

When I tell you, he checked everything off this impossible list, I couldn't believe it. I bought tickets to see my favorite transformational speaker live in Virginia. I had no idea who I was going to go with, but like I said, I was doing for myself what I wanted guys to do for me.

I asked Kevin if he wanted to come. After the show, I told him that this work is important to me, it had impacted my life so much and I feel like I need to keep going with it. I said he didn't have to be into it, but he'd have to support it.

At first, he wasn't into it and wasn't really into ghost/spirits. He had gone to Catholic private schools and wasn't super into all the stuff I was doing. He supported it though, I no longer was putting myself in a box to make other people like me more. If you can support what I do, even if you're not into it, then you can stay in my life.

This was my therapy; I don't go around bashing people in therapy. I actually felt this work was more effective than therapy because therapy brings things to the front of your awareness and generally doesn't tell you what to do with it and this work specifically gets that energy out of your body and moves it so that it's actually gone.

I told Kevin a lot about me, I made sure nothing could come out into the open later. Thank God, because it tried to come out. Kevin knew about my old life right away, he knew I sold my body in the past, he knew about E and about B.

At some point my relationship with Kevin triggered someone and it's debatable who after seeing what some of the people that used to be in my life were capable of. Someone took a photo from when I was with E and created a Facebook account for it. I was naked laying on top of an insane amount of money. They sent the photo to Kevin trying to tell him that I had a sugar daddy.

It was laughable really. I have always been the type of person to tell my partners my business. I had people before try to tell Alex that I was selling my body and he always laughed and said, "Who doesn't know that?"

The best way to be unbothered about other people's triggers is to always own your shit. People that I loved always knew who I was and what I was doing. There was no shocking my parents, my partners, the only thing I did was shelter my children from my past as long as I could.

I don't care who you are in the world, kids should stay out of disputes and shouldn't be involved in confrontations no matter how much you love the person, are angry with the person. Children are innocents and mom-guilt is a real depressive issue. If you wouldn't bring up someone having cancer in an argument do not bring up their kids. It's a low blow that doesn't need to happen. My rule of thumb is if it's not enough for CPS to get involved then it shouldn't be said, if it is enough for CPS to get involved then call CPS and you still shouldn't say it.

I am really firm about this because since everyone I loved knew who I was and what I was doing, they would always come for my kids. I was never a good enough mom. I carried this for so long. I carried it for so long because every confrontation with former friends, every time I didn't do something for someone else, every time I let someone down, they always came for my kids.

They'd tell me I was neglectful or mean, or even abusive. They'd conclude their own definition of what parenting should be and point out everything I did wrong or not enough of. People through my life have done this a lot because it was the only way to hurt me. My life was about my kids.

This book is focused on the spiritual aspects of my life and every situation from a spiritual perspective, but don't forget a second think I didn't go to court three different times for my kids to get full and totally custody back. Most of my life was based around the type of mom I should be for court and custody, most of the time I didn't feel like I had the freedom that others had to choose to use attachment parenting or go granola because every single thing you can do as a mother is going to have a downside and if I let anyone know my personal downside, it would be used in court.

That being said, not only did people come for my parenting to hurt my feelings but I didn't have the freedom to change it as I had changed so much else in my life. I felt suffocated by this and started to break free of it with Kevin by my side. In fact, the first time he met them he brough the stuff to cook dinner for them because I mentioned that I wanted to cook more meals for them.

Eventually, Kevin noticed how big of an impact this journey was making on my life. Over time he saw the growth. The beginning was very difficult because a lot of insecurities came up that I couldn't see when I was single. No matter how much inner work that you do alone, no matter what when you add another person it's going to surface more. We used to have a lot of conflict in the beginning, we argued a lot while I was analyzing what was coming up and how to release it.

Over time, monthly arguments turned to yearly arguments. We learned to communicate effectively together. He noticed that the more I released, the higher my vibration was and the more kind of magic I had access to. When we were struggling financially a bit, sometimes I would just come into big chunks of money. It happened more frequently the deeper I went into this connection.

6 THE SHEDDING

I spent time in this space really looking at my friends. I wanted more people like Kevin in my life, I wanted support and a tribe. I never had a girl group where we all hung out, I more had a different friend for each part of my personality and felt that I could never be loved for all of myself.

Now that I had a taste of that with one person, I wanted my whole life to be filled with that. Someone told me once that you are the average of your five closest friends. This is true on every level imaginable. The things you don't like about your two least favorite friends, you have those traits. Same with the things you love about all of your friends.

You have to be willing to risk losing everything to gain everything. The great Kyle Cease once said, "You're only ever as happy as you're willing to allow yourself to feel sad." This is another statement that ripples out through space/time. You have to take chances and I was willing to do that and see what happens next.

I cut off all my friends that weren't aligned. One of them didn't end well and I hadn't actually planned on ending at all. It happened organically because I was starting to find success in a lot of categories, and she couldn't celebrate me. What I did for others was celebrate the shit out of their success. I wanted celebration too, and I was realizing I am worthy of it. I never had a wedding, a baby shower, a celebration of any sort. She was removed for the lack of support I was getting versus the energy she was giving me. Everything should be equal energy exchange and if you're not keeping people in your life who give you the same energy you give them, that's enough reason to just bail. Yes, of course people go through stuff, but this was intentional, and you can tell if a person is this way by looking at the history of the relationship and listing out all of the things you have done for them and all of the things, they have done for you. If the page is obviously uneven, like very obviously, ditch it.

She then decided to go to one of my coaches after 6 months of not speaking to her and tell her about my past and the prostitution and how my coach should stop promoting me. She, herself, a woman's empowerment coach, going out of her way to try to tear down another woman. Again, my coach knew everything about me because I own what I have done, so nothing happened other than me knowing I made the right choice.

Fortunately, with my coach I met Spring. Spring was joining the course in order to build and better establish her online underwear business and I didn't really have a niche, but I wanted to learn about coaching, I felt because of my life I had a lot of experience to offer, and I could help a lot of people.

After a few months of working with my coach, Spring told me I had so many energetic and metaphysical experiences that I needed to learn how to connect at will. There was a woman that popped up in my life several times over the years that I wanted to learn from, but she was no longer teaching.

Spring told me to sit down and just learn within myself, force myself to figure it out like I had done so many other times in my life. I spent two weeks experimenting, in meditation, working almost nonstop on it. After two weeks I could do essentially anything that I wanted with energy. I wanted to know if there were truly intuitive people or if this was a skill anyone could have. So, then I told Spring we had to test it.

I was approaching it from the beginning from a research perspective, but when I ran through it with Spring all of her gifts opened up too, she was connecting and perceiving information in energy that she couldn't possibly have known. We began remote viewing each other, describing each other's homes when we had never been to them.

I didn't know if we were going insane or it was actually happening, so we took it further. We ran trial sessions on everyone we knew and similar to when I ran around asking guys out, we were totally petrified of the rejection. We didn't want to be wrong or look insane, but when you're afraid of something you have to do it anyway.

Just like before, we were never wrong.

Developing this energetic connection causes your overall frequency to raise even high than when you begin doing the work on yourself. Because of that we stopped aligning with that particular coach and group of people, but we did begin our own business together.

The thing I love about us is that we are constantly exploring this world, it never gets tiring. We explored spirits angels, dimensions, and one day I wanted to explore aliens.

Aliens, in theory, would only be able to access Earth through space/time by traveling through dimensions because otherwise it would take too long to travel. When you move through space, it takes time. But using that same comparison, you can move through time with space. Our physical bodies don't have this capacity, however our spirit, our consciousness does.

Connecting to aliens, or extra-dimensional living beings, got weird. Spring couldn't figure out if I was real at all because we had only interacted virtually and we both had experiences of dematerialization. The same experiences despite leaving out key specific details.

We shed the idea of being crazy. We had to stop using that word because it was bringing out a subconscious programming, a belief that alien people wore tin foil hats and belonged locked away. We started saying, "This magical thing just happened."

We had to accept that there were parts of this world that people had access to, and other people chose not to see, and just because one person decided to use access to it does not make them crazy. Trust me, I am in therapy and my therapist hasn't called the psyche ward yet.

At this point, no one can call me things I didn't personally experience about myself, so I am not afraid to share this section with you. I am not afraid of the conclusions you will draw or the beliefs you may project onto me.

I will tell you that I didn't sleep for three months during this time. It became difficult to talk to Kevin and Spring about what I was seeing and experiencing inter-dimensionally. I was terrified they would have me locked away, but I forced myself to stay open with them anyway. They never thought I was crazy, Spring was experiencing similar things and I was showing Kevin energies in the house that he could, in fact, also see.

We also had beings passing through that I tried to find in research. I saw a tall stickman one night, looked similar to slender man. I saw a tentacle thing. I am still between the tentacle thing being an actual thing or a form of really complex energetic technology. I had two abduction experiences, none of which were completely terrifying because I knew how to move my energy and astral body, I knew how to push back a little bit with practice.

West Virginia is actually one of the highest states with UFO and unexplained activity, much surpassing Roswell. That's where my mom went to be with her parents. When the COVID pandemic hit, my grandfather needed open heart surgery. Eventually, he was allowed to come home from a very lonely hospital visit, but he was dying.

I rushed down with my kids to be with him. We didn't spend a lot of time together in recent years, but he meant so much to me and I came to admire the life he led, wanting to mimic some of his lifestyle in my own.

I had a client and close friend perform reiki on the home while I was there, which changed the energy and allowed him to pass peacefully. There was so much pain with his passing, he was so loved and didn't want to leave us. There was just so much love with nowhere to go and it created this energy wound.

I saw his brother greet him on the other side when he passed, and I was there too. In space, time isn't linear. There is a point in time where we are not here, before we come or after we go. One of those versions of me also moved through time to be with him. There are some moments looking back where I wonder if I was actually guiding myself. The vision of me and the kids that told me to leave Alex, I always felt that was probably me.

After the funeral, I went back down, this time I took Kevin with me. As soon as he walked in the door a bag of my grandfather's favorite candy flew off the shelf and landed at Kevin's feet. The house is very active, it always had been. There's a magic in those mountains and I theorize it's because of a ley line or a vortex. I started experiencing other timelines when I was there.

I had memories, vivid memories, of my childhood that were not consistent with the memories and events of this reality that I was currently anchored in. The Mandela Effect, but with my own experiences.

My mom has had a best friend there since the dawn of time. I had significant memories of her husband passing away years and years ago. I would ask her daughter what it was like to not have a dad and if she was okay. When I went back with Kevin, I found out her husband has passed very recently and probably sounded like an insane person.

When I opened up to the small-town people there about some of my experiences, they don't usually have an opportunity to talk about it because there is so much judgement in small town life, but they began telling me their stories too. My grandmother even participated in instances where she went out with her friends and lost hours on the quick drive home, another very common theme among abductees.

7 EXPERIENCES

One night I woke up in the middle of the night and saw a little girl. She was about my daughter's age, so I jumped up thinking that it was, in fact, my daughter but just like that she was gone. I remember her hair being longer, straighter and darker so I started connecting with answers and finally I learned about the hybrid children.

The hybrid children are really cool, they're kind of our spirit children, or energy children. They learn about us, and they are kind of a team for us. There's so much that goes on right on top of us. It's worlds on top of worlds on top of worlds.

Another night, I woke up and saw Alex holding our daughter. I rubbed my eyes fully expecting it to go away. You know how you first wake up and maybe see something that isn't there and you blink a couple of times or rub your eyes and they anchor into reality better? That didn't happen this time. I saw someone standing there holding my daughter and so my response was to throw a pillow at the person because I knew it wasn't here.

At that moment he was gone, and Aurelia woke up immediately after. He held her for a month in my womb, but never got to meet her so that was sentimental. I always had dreams about him holding my miscarried baby and showing her to me.

I was able to explore the dream reality more too. I think sometimes when we dream it's messages from within us but sometimes, we go to a communal space. Not like astral projecting, but instead like a dream dimension or reality.

A space where our loved ones can visit us, and we can also visit each other. A space where the faces of people we don't know are real faces of people living.

Years ago, I had a dream of a psychic giving readings in a bar, and I walked up to her and asked for a reading, or she came up to me and asked to give me a reading. I always thought that was interesting because we were in the bar. I remembered her face completely and came across someone who knew her and set me up with a session. She was actually a psychic, same accent, same hair, same teeth even. She had no memory of traveling to my dream, but I saw her.

This year, I took a nap at the same time as one of my clients which just happened to happen because of the different time zones, we had a dream of each other in the same setting with others around. Our events were pretty closely synchronized in the dream.

The shamans talk about a collective dream and an individual dream and at first, I believed they talked about how we created our own personal experience here on Earth and then collectively create the whole experience. Now I am wondering if that is both literal and rippling out. What's on the micro is on the macro, right?

During mediumship sessions through my business, I have unknowingly channeled people who are alive but in a comatose state. I think this is similar to me meeting my grandfather on the other side, because there's a point in space/time where I can go back or forward and do that. It could be that they just simply aren't as connected to their body and they kind float around as spirit guides in the meantime I don't know. That's actually happened several times though and I never thought to ask one how that works.

I joined some online communities where people would practice their psychic skill and mediumship skill and I was scrolling through one day and saw a picture of a woman. I kept scrolling and suddenly spirit told me to go back, I'm listening to my intuition when it doesn't make sense remember?

I look through the comments under her picture and no one is saying they are getting her mother and I am totally getting her mother. I comment and I say hey, I don't know if you lost your mother, but I am feeling super strongly that I have your mother. She messaged me.

I asked her if she was struggling with fertility or conceiving, and her mother wanted to let her know it was going to be okay and she was going to have a baby. We became really good friends, and she became a long-term client developing her own abilities. I believe we are brought to people for a reason.

B was in my life to take me straight to Kevin because I would have kept that job forever. E was in my life to show me business and how to run business, and make sure I anchored into the type of business owner I wanted to be. Alex, he taught me so much I don't know where to begin and I continue to learn and grow through his parents to this day. Sometimes I felt like creating our daughter was his last mission here on Earth, what he came to do what completed and his time here was always meant to end right there. He dreamed it years before it every happened.

Spring and I have stayed up late channeling our living animals, asking why the dog eats the cat shit and why the cat does what it does. We would play games and google what we channeled to see if it's a common animal behavior.

Kevin would walk me up his family tree and I would channel the people that passed on from his family and give validations for them. I had to call his mom one night and insist that she give his grandfather's wedding ring to someone specific. The most beautiful part about this is that

I am no longer afraid to be who I am anymore, and it no longer denies me the authentic love that I deserve.

When I first started teaching Spring, I will never forget, I asked her if she had specifically stacked antique luggage or knew someone that did. She sent back a photo of her stacked antique luggage décor that belonged to her late father-in-law. The symbol in my head looked like a load of cartoon stacked luggage, cartoon meaning not only like someone drew it, but it was also piled in such a way that it could never actually be carried. Low and behold she had stacked antique luggage. I validated this whole spirit, and she was so blown away, just for him to tell her she had to clean the gutters.

It can be something so seemingly silly, it can bring their personality out, they can be jokesters or pranksters, or cleaning the gutters could actually prevent something terrible from happening so I choose to listen all the time now. Every time I don't, something terrible blows up so I'm firm on listening to what I get.

Something I've learned through this process is that free will is the most upheld law in all of the universe. We can find evidence that vaccines are safe or not safe, that the Earth is flat or round, that plants and animals have souls. This is the same when it comes to scary metaphysical experiences. Have I had scary shit happen? Fuck yes, but was it bad or evil? Absolutely not.

I have seen beings that look terrifying give me good news, I have seen someone's spine getting cut open because their brother was getting spinal surgery. I have been afraid more of the possibility that something could be bad rather than actually experiencing something "bad."

I have helped many women and men develop and none of my clients have had a scary experience happen that has led to any curse, attachment, evil.

Now, I'm not saying that the law of duality doesn't exist, that would be absurd. I'm saying the law of duality is an experienced perspective. I didn't expect to bring up perspective so much, but this is my experience. When I believe something is bad or evil, my mind instantly finds all the possibilities that could arise and all of the potentially evil things about it. This is how the brain works. If you're scared, your brain will hyper focus on everything scary. Ever heard the phrase, "Don't think, just jump." If you feel an emotion and then choose to think, your brain wants to justify the energy coming up.

I found this to be true, and it is one key component into how I leaped into so many chances, and I have found it to be true in the metaphysical world as well. We are supported, if we choose to be.

One morning I woke up and saw a large, very large, Egyptian person walk into my office. I got out of bed, and I followed it inside. My office was empty, but I saw down to connect. Thoth, coming through and asking for permission to upgrade my energy body to receive the information and connections I was trying to access for a particular project I was working on. I said absolutely, duh. Free will prohibits access to changing your energetic body without permission. How does this work with abductions you ask? They aren't altering you; they're doing something else entirely.

After this interaction with Thoth, I got worried. I got in my head thinking, "I'm doing all this work and teaching others to connect and teaching others to provide this and collapse time and space. What if I am on the wrong side?"

I declared to all of the metaphysical energy around me that I wasn't going any further or doing anymore practice until I knew who I was working for. I laid around my house until late at night when I started to drift to sleep when I saw my guides standing in a circle around me, pushing energy toward me and moving me up.

I kept getting pushed up by level after level of energy, from my guides, to extra-dimensionals, to ascended masters. Above layers of angels and then I was floating in a place that had the most beautiful golden clouds I had ever seen. I was lucid, I was not asleep, but I was not in my body anymore. It was the same as one of those visions but this time I was consciously in it. That's when I heard it.

8 SOURCE

I wasn't a God person. I was always into movies like Practical Magic and shows like Charmed.
In fact, when I saw spiritual people use the term God instead of source, I used to cringe and sometimes even unfollow and delete.

I had clients who were raised on the bible, and I always politely listened and observed, Spring was an ex-Mormon, and she supported my lack of God stuff. I didn't really have an opinion I just knew church people weren't usually my jam. People construct God to be whatever their need from God is at the time, must like they do with the people in their lives. I just thought that God was a commonly used excuse to be an asshole.

Boy, was I wrong.

I heard this booming loud voice come through and I knew who it was. I have never experienced anything like that. Not before and not since then. I knew the work I was doing was on the right side, so I went back to work and that was that.

The discussion between me and The Creator was not in depth so you're not missing much. My initial emotional reaction was pretty, "Oh my god, I didn't mean to disturb you I'm so sorry." I can tell you that there weren't emotions like I was having. That wasn't funny or cute or disturbing. God just IS.

I felt really curious as to why I am so important that I would get a call when I threatened to stop working. I also asked myself if that was my ego because we are all pretty important.

Things started to make a little more sense though. People always say the bible is a metaphor, but I don't think it is. I think the vibration of the planet was higher when there was less access to materialism and egoic nature and I think a lot of people were actually channels. Do I think the church altered shit to feed the narrative? Yes, it's totally proven. The oldest bible is in Arabic, translated it contains over 3000 edits from the NKJ bible today.

The oldest bible contains the Old Testament in its entirety and parts of the New Testament. The bible itself has a name- The Codex Sinaiticus.

I did my God research after that one.

When you snap out of this day to day living and connect with the universal energy on a deeper level you start seeing things that matter substantially more than bullshit jobs, rent, fad diets and drama with the Kardashians. You start to notice that we live in a solar system and have this complex recipe for life on our planet, where the planet probably began with one cell organisms and grew the way little worm parasites grow in a glass of water if you leave it outside long enough, and over years and years those little, tiny organisms grew to animals, species based on the environment they lived, plats and this perfected ecosystem where everything needs everything to survive. This oneness of both independence and dependence.

When you look outside of our planet you don't know if other planets have this compound, you can't see very far but you can theorize that based on the planet's core and position, and general compound that if another planet did grow life, it will look different, interact differently and depend on different nutrients, gasses, etc. When it comes to God, or source, you wonder if everything is just here, layers of dimensions right on top of us. Are we all centrally located and have been coexisting all along?

I started thinking more about how this life was so miraculous that I didn't want to spend another second doing anything that didn't feel good. It's not worth a life of misery just to do what makes you fit. I worked my whole life for stability and normalcy only to come to a space where, if I knew this before, I'd buy an RV instead, throw my kids in and travel. I'd build connections instead of collections, but it is never too late to begin.

Now it just looks a little different, but whether you're 18 or 88, there is never a reason to spend the rest of your years under the thumb of anymore, crushing yourself smaller and smaller to fit in a box. No one's box is worth it, not one person's and definitely not society's.

9 BEGIN WITH THE BRAIN

When I was living across the country, after Alex died, I needed to start this process of internal reflection. I found transformational speakers on YouTube and began feeding my brain as much as possible.

The ones that help you integrate the work are the ones who typically show you them talking to people on stage or pulling people on the call so that you can see the excuses and see how they're broken down and integrated.

I began a meditation routine, sometimes I think of my brain as a pet I have to train because it's so easily conditioned and a pattern recognition machine. Let me explain.

When you are driving and you come to consciousness and don't realize how you got where you are, you somehow are where you needed to go but you haven't been present for the entire drive, I call that autopilot. When your brain goes into autopilot, the conscious mind takes a backseat, and the subconscious takes over because you're doing something very routine. You probably do this for drives to work or somewhere that you go very regularly. This is a space of channeling. Another good example is the shower. You do the same thing, in the same order, every single time you take a shower. You might get creative ideas in the shower or jump out and need to make a post or call someone. This is because your conscious took a backseat, and you channeled the idea.

Meditation is rough, so I teach people a routine to help train their brain in a very short time (if done every day) to settle into a state of channeling. An example that I often use is to light a candle, burn some sage, and play the same music.

After a few days, your brain will know that when it sees the flame, feels the heat, smells the smell and hears the music that it is time to settle in and channel. You're activating your physical sensory system in a routine way every single day. Like when you house train a dog and it knows if it pees outside it gets a treat. See? Your brain is a pet.

We are not our bodies and I think that's so important. You don't actually look like you do in your spaceship that is carrying you around this world. We have to learn to program our spaceships in an effective way to live quality and connected lives here.

Are there really aliens or just alien parts of us that we need to accept and become one with? Because if you think in the sense of our physical reality, the life we live on a day-to-day basis is an absolute construct of our internal selves then that could be true.

An example of this might be someone who wants to be accepted, so he has a ton of friends and does everything he thinks his friends will want him to be to accept him. This is because he can't accept himself. The internal conflict is not accepting the self enough to show it to the world, and it manifests physically by having a lot of friends and always wanting to be something for them. It ripples even further too. Maybe this guy wants to be accepted so badly, that the friends use him or think he's annoying and further take action to push him away and make him feel even less accepted.

This happens with every single thing in our lives. Our

physical reality mirrors back to us what isn't in alignment on the inside in every single situation possible. If you aren't living a life of joy and you want to, take note of why your life isn't joyous and compare it to the same emotions on the inside. Journaling helps so you can see it in your face. I just prompt myself with questions about my feelings.

One time, I was super annoyed with a friend. She could afford an apartment and a car, but she was too terrified to break into independence and inconvenienced everyone else to move through life. In the spiritual world, there's nothing wrong with this girl, I have the problem. Let me explain.

What someone else does in absolutely no way, shape, or form has any effect on my life. If it does have an effect on my life, I can create boundaries or remove these people from my life. For someone else's decision making in their life to bother me, that is 100% something wrong inside of me.

My specific problem with this specific person was that I was starting my business and I was afraid to come out of the spiritual closet and tell my ghost stories and have people think I lost my damn mind and be a failure. See? Nothing to do with her. I was angry at my reflection inside of her. Scared to take a leap of faith for myself when I know that it's the best thing for me. I was annoyed with her because she was scared to take a leap for herself even though she knew it was the best thing for her.

Advice isn't even advice. I get carried away giving advice sometimes and I feel really bad for it because my advice is always for me. I can only give advice based on my perspective and experience so the only person the advice is good for is me. I'm projecting advice on to you. Have you ever told someone to quit their job, when you, in fact, hate your job? Yeah, that was your subconscious talking to you. Ever told someone to leave their significant other when you were, in fact, unhappy? You guessed it, that was for you.

All that's left to do from this point is integrate actually listening to yourself. I try, and fail epically sometimes, but I do try to give people their power back when they ask me for advice. When people ask for advice they want validation, and they usually already know what they want to do and don't have the confidence. Just lend support and ask them what they feel, want, whatever. It won't affect you if you're not projecting anyway.

10 REALITY

As I previously mentioned, abundance would also be an internal perception manifested into the physical reality. Ever wonder why douchebags end up wealthy? Because they're abundant and deserving perception of themselves cannot be altered.

Millions of people did not believe that Donald Trump could become president, but he believed it and that was enough. He believed it so much, that other people believed him because he was so sure. That reality then became a shared reality. A collective reality.

Have you ever spent a lot of time with someone and shared a lot of their perspectives and beliefs and started having also the same issues in your life? You can move through and exist in the reality of others based on your beliefs, thoughts and perceptions synchronizing with theirs. Time alone is really important so that you can settle, connect and anchor into the reality you choose to live in, you can just create it. Free will and the parts of us connected to source allow us to create.

My reality doesn't look the same as a lot of people's reality and so my life doesn't hold the same binds and rules. You can shift, you can create new, you can link into someone else's. When we aren't creating our own reality, we are a character in someone else's though. I think it's important to anchor on what you want to create because when we aren't creating, we are free-falling and land wherever and it's not always a soft landing.

There are infinite possibilities, directions, things to create. There are a million different roads to get to where you want to go, and you have the freedom to choose the road or hang a tight left and explore something else. Wherever you go, whatever you choose, just do it intentionally.

ABOUT THE AUTHOR

Cossondre is a Psychic Medium & Spiritual Leader. Also known as The Mystic from The Mystic and The Magician Podcast, she works with intention to inspire the world and help raise the vibration and teach about energy and connection.

Social Media
IG
@Cossondre
Facebook Community
www.facebook.com/groups/modernmysticsandmagicians
Podcast
The Mystic and The Magician
Email
Cossondre.Anderson@icloud.com